Nurdles

and Other Poems

by

Allison A. deFreese

Finishing Line Press
Georgetown, Kentucky

Nurdles
and Other Poems

To Daniel

ACKNOWLEDGMENTS

I am grateful to the following publications in which versions of the individual poems
in this chapbook first appeared:

Bangalore Review, "Flashback, The Gorge"
Beyond Words Literary Magazine, "Honey"
Cathexis Northwest Press, "Colonies" and "Fragments"
Dendro Ediciones Perú: *Aislados · Dosis de poesía para tiempos inciertos*, "Colonias"
        (original poem written in Spanish)
Ember Chasm Review, "Currents"
Eunoia Review, "Haze," "Judgment," "Morels," "Nurdles," and "The Words"
Fireweed: Poetry of Oregon: "To My Neighbor"
Hunger Mountain, "Delight"
Plainsongs, "Restraint"
La Piccioletta Barca, "Strains;" and "Scales in A Minor" (previously, "On Moss and
        Memory")
Midway Journal, "On Swallows"
New York Quarterly, "Showings"
2020 Oregon Poetry Society Anthology, "Strains"
River Heron Review, "Unearthings"
South Dakota State Poetry Society, "Amber," "April 26, 2026 (51.2763° N, 30.2219° E),"
        and "Porch Light"
Southword (Munster Literature Centre, Ireland), "Flashback, Arrangement for a
        Warm Place"
Typishly Literary Magazine, "The Act of Singing"

Publisher: Leah Huete de Maines
Editor: Christen Kincaid
Cover Art: Detail from "Wild Strawberries" by Dorota Haber-Lehigh
Author Photo: Imagen Congreso (Mérida, Yucatán)
Cover Design: Elizabeth Maines McCleavy

Order online: www.finishinglinepress.com
        also available on amazon.com

Author inquiries and mail orders:
Finishing Line Press
PO Box 1626
Georgetown, Kentucky 40324
USA

Table of Contents

On Swallows

And an upthrust of feathers
before the downpour
darting downcloud from grey cumuli
still gilded and glowing—
growing weather ahead
as the last light settles in
low through rafters
under tin—
in the midship of the shed,
their stucco nests.
And swallows swing starboard
ascending above the side yard
to catch gnats
that flex in currents
beyond the curtain—
before switching swift to port
to dive for mosquitos
more dangerous than lions.

Delight

For Lora

It's been so long
since I've fed a horse an apple;
I've nearly forgotten
the swan neck foaming
under the comb,
the flicker in the nostrils
like a gentle dragon,
her nicker, and that the muzzle
grazing my hand
was the softest thing created.
The curled lip extending
above the plateau of teeth,
the mare accepting the apple
in my palm
and the fruit exploding
in a white nectar mist
over the whisper
of whiskers on the chin.

My bangs grown long
into my eyes now,
in the luminous light of pre-evening,
I am blinking like a pony
across the gate
into the gaze
of a forgotten tree
at the end of the neighborhood.
It is bursting with apples
and dancing with summer bees.
Here there are no horses,
the fruit falls abandoned,
rolling into the grass
and shrinking.

A little longer
and I'll catch
my hair back in a band,
hold it behind my ears
and clip it above my forehead.

After months without a trim
or weeding,
I'll be neat again
like a fjord horse shorn
or a jumper's mane
buttoned and restrained,
as a horse I cannot see
stomps and snorts—
shakes loose from its tether
and perhaps spreads its wings
in late afternoon air
that smells like sweet cider,
the apples shriveling,
the ground alive with butterflies.

The Words

I.

When the words
arrived in the world this time
even the largest survived—
behemoths and heffalumps
lumbering down deserted highways
between forest and skyscrapers—
the lightest drifting the city
in halos of pollen,
lifting quick and birdlike,
riding bees' legs
into a hagiographic haze—
an orange cat on the saffron balcony,
bathing the sunset in whiskers.

II.

And the words thrived in silence
alone, whispered, quiet.

III.

To congregate once meant
a chorus,
a flocking cacophony;
cocks crowing in a crowd—
the crows on the rooftops tossing twigs into the air
as if rolling dice.

IV.

Am I late?
Is it the nightingale or the lark?

V.

It was spring.
A virus bloomed in the nose and throat.
Ghee turned to gold

in the mouth
of the universe—
a dream of cows in the vacuum,
vaccinating the void
of milky thin days
with mold on toast.

Honey

To my niece

The sunflower is already the sun—
there is nothing to change
in its paper doll mane,
in the whorl
steadily turning,
and as always toward the light.
And the bee
is already a honey tiger
rising with resin
over fields of dandelion,
gold flowers that know,
though never told,
to spread and shine,
and fly—seeds lifting
skyward with no need of wings,
drifting away on pollinators
that are already the honey
in the two blonde chaps
they wear on their legs—
those tiny pollen baskets.
The buff hen in the side yard
carries our whole solar system
of amber eggs under her plumes,
from smallest to solid;
the weathervane
rotating with its rooster.
And you, already perfect,
in a unicorn T-shirt
of rainbow on seahorse,
already the unique person
you will always be
beyond the braid of genes,
or synchronized lines of geese.
You grow, expanding
with waves from the source,
with the stars' blue flames
within you, the glow from the first explosion,
the light of the first yolk rising.

To My Neighbor

Gina, you can keep
the green vases
from the daffodils.
My hyacinths
have long since shriveled
but tulips burgeon
in the beds by the steps
and soon iris will rise.
I can see them through the window
where I'm smiling
and waving to you.
Why not come across the street
and pick them; they are yours.
The vases are, too,
did I say that? My mind's circling—
I don't want them back on this side.
It's been a strange season,
yes, and you are welcome!
Just don't breathe near me
and I don't want to see you
any closer than this, behind glass,
underwater, the stems in the vases;
please do cut a nice bouquet anyway
since I can't take them to my mother.

Currents

I have known too many
who have drowned—
the brothers tanned and warned
of the Marais des Cygnes's
twisting eddies,
their inner tubes taken anyway
past the sandbar;
or the town teens
younger than a cicada's cycle
dragged into brackish galaxies
while spanning the Kansas on a dare,
and college friends tossed
from their raft in rapids,
lost on the Kaw in Shawnee;
the divers sent to find them
said catfish bigger than men
swam the muddy bottom, fish
that might pull you under
if the river didn't. Decades later,
the ones swept away
from us with flooded lungs—
my father floating
in his hospital bed,
his bronchi branching
underwater
after hitting a final snag.

Unearthings

To my brother

I set aside my spade.
From under the over-wintering favas
I've dug up a giant potato
from another summer—
a catfish with white whiskers
flopping in the bottom
of the boat, my brother
and I holding bamboo poles.
The prize is his, our biggest,
though once I hooked
an alligator snapper
that broke free.
We are eight and nine,
shaded by trees in calm water
drifting back to when the world was milk—
our father not yet ash,
none of the grandparents
planted at New Basel.
We are too young to wonder:
Does the air sting
a fish's skin after the water has broken?
Does a baby's first breath burn?
Did our father's final inhale?
And how does a seed feel
the first night submerged
in soil? Worms inhumed
in loam; the new cover beans
buried in this bed only last week,
are already unwinding,
an embryo in darkness.

Flashback, The Gorge

The summer of the eclipse, the Gorge was burning. Little boats of ash sailed down from a caramel sky, as if Pompeii, as if Krakatoa on the morning of The Scream. But here was silence, not catastrophe, just the strange still of songbirds gathered without a sound on the dry green, as if children between gasps at a recess where there is no play, the building sent out for a drill turned real—at the edge of a suburb where dark farms still cling to a city nightscape, fields sown with nothing to be eaten, a pumpkin patch or a corn maze, ten miles outside the fire evacuation line. And elsewhere—later as we slip on our solar shades and watch the moon's umbra quench the stars—stand the cows, up to their necks in a flooded pasture, the horses whinnying in flames a state away, circling a smoky corral. Yes, we know: the world is safe, and this year was only anomaly.

Nurdles

Larger than germ or virus,
smaller than thistle seed for finches—
these grains feed nothing,
nourish no one.
Mermaid tears washed
ashore
into our salt bowls,
discrete as hot spring amebae
or bright as cascarón confetti
hatched at Pascua, a resin
of beached rice rolled
round as roe
for a November 2nd wedding,
the guests masked in marigolds.
We micro-dose fine synthetics
from our first breath,
their invisible quills
lodging in sponge tissue;
breathable polyurethane—
smooth as swan boats
on Chapultepec or Ueno—
tugged into the wailing belly
from the binky or bottle.
Tasteless, they flavor
our applesauce, ingested
in the first solid spoonful,
in bread, butter, honey.
On the inside
from the beginning
we are intimate with them—
with these microfibers
the wild plastic
blowing through my hair
after a windy ride over oceans
that swallow cities as they rise.

One day I will tell children
raised on such formulas
what I remember of songbirds,

fish and fresh water—
black sand holding nothing
more than traces of gold—
and how once, out the window,
we saw bees, flowers, trees.

Flashback, Arrangement for a Warm Place

Yes, please send me the orchids
a bird-of-paradise too
and two fuchsias,
coconut oil lightly toasted
with a mouthful of saltwater
sneezed through the nose,
butterflies and bees
tarred in their own
wildsweet honey.
And yes, please throw
in the cockroach-under-the-bed,
older than us all and enduring eternities—
minds her-his-its own business mostly,
popping out for mango scraps
or muffin crumb. I never
had the heart to take
a swat at it, about its shiny business
roaching things about   bold
and slow maneuvering
the rattan, the linoleum—
doesn't know it's a roach really
thinks it's mine—or me from another time.
Send it back through the centuries—
hand-delivered, one to outlast
all the flowers, traveling still—
in the lining of a suitcase
between the dinner trays
in the foil of your flowerpot
stowaway.

Strains

If we can now freeze genes,
why not write a book of snow
on a field lain fallow
and read it
to pumpkin seeds
that hold pumpkins in their raspy husks—
though birdseed
does not sprout sparrows,
regardless of the strain—
and a baby made of milk
does not resemble the opaque narrative
of lactation, nor the Milky Way;
a book of tapioca
for the frogs with their wealth of tadpoles
grazing the reeds and rushes
about the gladiolas turned lanterns
after pages of rain
and the rabbit's ear, transparent,
illuminated in the sunset.
The sunflowers
have gone to seed now
without a hint of yellow.
The horse has feathers
but cannot fly,
and drops of rain,
once fallen—run into one water,
both fresh and older than our sun.

And then the monarch turns a page,
after straining
out of its chrysalis
and drying its crackled panes
before rising softly
on solid wings—
once locked in a whole note
on milkweed leaf,
then a striped caterpillar,
and finally turning to liquid
in the pupa—
strands of silk twisting
sheet music.

Fragments

And what if we lost only
what we don't need?
Two thousand years later
         Sappho still stands
  with her lopped hands
  her nose gone long ago.
She is blanched like a brain of coral
           in a red tide
    after the glaciers turn to lace

more perfect than ever today
in her minimalism—
closed and polished,
even the hint of lips
erased.
      Her words stood time too
                in   fragments
      enough
soul
           there
      to take our breath away
         to return a pulse
         a millennia later
         and shock the heart back
                after it has been pronounced
fragile.

Showings

Seven centuries back
our Lady
of Norwich
found the cosmos
in her palm
without washing
her hands first.
The fever broke;
the universe expanded,
spinning on a spangled axis.
Inside the hazelnut
she held in her hand—
in the cranium-smooth
brown shell—were the ridges
of everything that was,
that had ever been.

How could she know
a sneeze
can sac a city—
as can mosquito larvae
twitching
with the moon
gone yellow
in the bottom
of a well—
a rat's tail
passing in the night
with the comet's trail.

Amber

To Frida again

I wanted to talk to you
about the honey again
because news from the hive
is always so good and golden—
because 4000-year-old honey
sealed with the Bee Kings of Egypt
is still fresh and live in Luxor—
because after five millennia in Tbilisi
honey from the catacombs was still intact,
though slightly crystalized—
because there are meliponines in Mérida,
stingless Mayan bees,
though even ones with stingers act once,
then fall on their own swords—
because a virus may bloom
in a coin purse, but bacteria
cannot land long in this liquid gold,
not even once you've licked the spoon
flowing with spun honey
finer than thread for a tapestry—
because bees drift over globe thistles,
love-in-a-mist, baby's breath
and snapdragons, until at last entering
a foxglove—or a monkshood in royal, not saffron:
Their humming soothes
with the purr of the universe
mellifluous as baklava
as milkweeds and mead;
a wolf of bees
swiping the swarm from a stump
downed hollow in a storm,
or the low drone from pyramids
of roasted grain preserved
in summer honey
in topaz and amethyst—
because if you leave a slice
for the Queen,
you can eat honey with melted butter
and not kill anything

while nurse bees
feed their brood jelly
by the bottom board
under the drone combs.

Judgment

For years I was anonymous,
nearly invisible.
No one ever reported me
on my morning jogs
for running from something
I must have done;
no one followed me through Plaid Pantry
to see what I'd shove in my purse next;
no one ever took me into a backroom
at the mall to search my bag,
surprised when the tampon and lipstick
rolled out, to find a woman under the hoodie.
I've never been accused of doing anything more
than birdwatching when I watch birds;
never been maced for looking in a bike shop window
because someone thought I was casing the place
when I needed patches
and a cycle was my only ride to school
or choked on a cafeteria floor,
the penalty, death, for throwing a sandwich.
I've never been thrown
against the side of a squad car,
never cuffed on concrete, throttled
at the neck, my face cracking on pavement,
though cops have stopped me
in rural Kansas for driving with Oregon plates,
called in the K-9 unit
had me pop the trunk.

How surprised they were
to find only a typewriter back there,
recoiling from the sight of it
as if discovering a cargo of snakes,
as if expecting an explosion.
Still, at most this was annoyance;
I didn't fear they would cuff me,
suffocate me, plant something on me
and take me away. My mother
was not incarcerated
for the first nine years of my life

and I didn't lose my father in a raid.
During the school lockdown event,
when the flak jackets and AKs
burst in to save us,
I put my hands up and I was saved.
There were students, though,
more frightened of this display
than of any threat that lay waiting outside
in the familiar.
Here, the first moment of panic
after hours in there—
though we had been locked
in the classroom from the beginning,
and done nothing—
they tried to run
out the backdoor,
to reach the street
where there was air to fly,
where they knew they could still breathe.

April 26, 2026 (51.2763° N, 30.2219° E)

      and forever after it is summer where apples cannot be eaten
and cucumbers ripen in the shadow of untouchable green.

      no ambulance in forty years to pierce the empty streets, the
tumbril of silence and slow time in a world where nothing human
putrefies or petrifies or can profit.

      then elk return with silken flanks to silver birch and hornbeam
and the boar and bear breed and breathe, and foxes rustle the red forest
again stepping over gentians that are whispering to the swallows with
uneven beaks:

                         little town by river in spring—

                         Cold Eden

The Act of Singing

To Marilyn, Neva, Erwin

Maybe only birds
are safe now
as they pipe up
with their dry voices
or perhaps the dragonfly
drying its mosaic wings
in silence on the door screen.
Even the fish that keep surfacing,
though so briefly—
shifting shape as they ripple
beneath water patterns and leaves—
stay far from the warm mist
of conversation. If so,
then we must keep singing
anyway, alone, away from words
projected deep or carried airborne.
We must mask and muzzle
if we wish to breathe,
play our piano solos solo
as if entering single digits
into an adding machine,
or reading a secret note
in the invisible ink
of a dream.
A flat or sharp—
a whole note floating
like a U.F.O.
or held
like a trilobite
in limestone,
the trebles twisting
in their trembling script
as F-clefs bat their lashes
near your own ear
whistling like half a wishbone.
The choirs have folded
like music boxes,
snapped closed like fans
only to reappear again

online, a cappella
on a flat screen—
the parched scream for the queen
of the night, lone nightingale
whose grace is amazing.

Colonias

Así que esta mañana
las hormigas entran
por debajo del ventanal
a través de una grieta—
un agujero en el universo—
cuya luz ilumina el polvo
de mil millones de años.
Reunidas en el sereno
santuario del ábside
de la corteza de pan
de masa madre
dejada con descuido
en la encimera—
la hogaza abovedada,
la masa ya leudada
y levantada del molde
justo a tiempo para el té
con la mantequilla—
la rebanada perforada
la miga embelesada de burbujas.
Desde la mesa
yo también siento
la textura arenosa
de pan tostado en la lengua
aspiro, mastico
y esto significa
que he despertado otra vez
y como la congregación
minúscula y sin remisa
vivo todavía—
mientras las migajas
más vastas que casas
ya salen en silencio hacia el sol.

Colonies

And so this afternoon
the ants return
with the billion-year dust
caught in sunlight.
They have entered
through a gap
under the window,
a hole in the universe.
Communing
on the counter,
their sanctuary
the apse of this sourdough,
a wafer-thin slice
carelessly left there,
the vaulted loaf
having risen in the tin
just in time
for tea and butter—
crust pierced
crumb raptured with bubbles.
They would carry me off
too, little visitors
were they able,
our worlds distant
as trees and paper,
as Heaven or blue Neptune.
At the table, I, too,
sense bread again,
the gritty texture
of toast on tongue—
I smell and swallow;
and this means
I am
like the small congregation
awake and still
among the living
as breadcrumbs
the size of houses
leave silently in a line.

Scales in A Minor

After Leonard Cohen's speech in Asturias

All night
a ghost with six fingers
has been sweeping
these same polydactyl chords
into a broken French in the corner.
The leap at the end was long and wingless,
feather light and heavenly
as the tremolo in a storm's breath.
Did he waiver as he jumped the 6th,
as arpeggios and legatos
skipped and bent? The rosette
fragrance that rose from the case later
filled a space round and full as Oviedo,
beginning and ending in an *Oh!*
open to infinities and interpretation
or scattered over ocean.
His guitar filled then with helium,
high and weightless waves
awakened with the vibration
of notes at last floating
into dimensions of gratitude
drifting, then, in the direction
of delirium or dementia
where forgotten scales crest and break
with harmony and minor hauntings
in the grain of living wood
picked vivid and unsleeping under strings,
the roots—music unfretted in soil or soul.
The sap kept stiff in the trunk
quickens all winter while leaves
are already assembling in the buds,
tucked tight as birds waiting to wail.
What might have happened,
you might ask, had you played
for him back then as you could at the end:
with a skyward twitching in the wings
or slow as moss twisting upward
and over a green stone
where fern fronds inquire and ask
the unanswerable, bending into questions
as they uncurl?

Haze

eventually one must come to love
        the uncertainty at the edges where the universe crumbles
                into cake glaze just as the ants are arriving,
        when the plates shift
                    and a row of houses
                            hangs now only by a foundation
fragile as the threads of milk teeth and the second grade.

faith smarts like bleach when you breathe in
        even as you cling to the cliff
                where boats and sea beasts
                          swim off a flat planet
      into milky galaxies
      when glaciers calve.

planes drift the ocean,
            ships float a sky gone red
            and ashen with forest falling over iceberg lace
      and the gray coral of the brain.
when the floods do recede
            boas or mold may arrive
                with the peace olives and wings.

yet there are orchids in your veins—
            secret sugars quickening in the blood
            a seashell spooled in your inner ear.
      there was no chance of creation
from the scent of that salty beginning.
      your mind the vessel
            of nebulas and navigations
                and more than all infinity.

catch your breath!
      the dove that had landed
            is soaring again
        with the birds from a sand dollar
      in the clouds of your tissue, in your waters:
                            hummingbird nectar

            pink sunsets

                      carambola blossoms

        abalone

                    a sort of euphoria

Porch Light

This was the best theater
when I was seven or nine
or even thirteen and sixty
miles south of Kansas City—
this porch where we sat
when the warm months
folded their wings
around the farmhouse
on a gravel backroad—
the sky spackled with stars
even with our light on,
the Milky Way curling into the night,
as cottonwoods and milkweeds
released their airy seed.
In the humid hum of summer
cicadas and a whippoorwill
from the woods, fireflies
drifted over a dusky pasture
where soon constellations would rise,
flickering as they burned,
while planets signaled to us
with a single solid beacon.

And under the porchlight,
such life—a rhinoceros
like the back of a polished banister;
a two-point stag beetle
moving into the strobe,
magical as an elk
in an old-growth forest;
weevils with inflexible noses
pacing the stage as a walkingstick
without a shadow
stretched long like something from Alice.
Sometimes a Japanese June bug
with its broach in iridescent jade
would clasp the screen door
or a pill bug tuck its legs under
like an armadillo the size of a car
awakened in the excavation of a dry riverbed.
And one night, during the meteors

appeared a Luna moth, illuminated—
at the tip of my finger,
a kite of eyes and coattails
feathery as felt and green
as a gentle dragon.

It was under this light
they carried me that evening
as I came back into consciousness
after falling from Lucky Lady,
thrown—no one had known
she once showed at rodeos—
and shined flashlights into my eyes
in search of a concussion.
It was there where our neighbor
came over late so my brother and I
could see the limp coyote
he'd hit in the pickup—
holding it in both arms
like a sleeping child.

Morels

Once we would wander
through forest clouds
canopy green
over river dapplings.
My brother and I scanning
the understory for ancient edibles
elusive mycelium
honeycombed and amber
with dark olive catacombs
for springtails or snails.

Morel spores outlasting
our grandparents,
outliving all that's mortal—
dissipating through history
before the branch
from common ancestors
before the first rings
formed inside trees.
We'd find their spires rising low,
in the abandoned orchard
that once tolled
with windfalls of apples,
their steeples lifting sails
of damp leaves under ash
and Osage orange,
or shaded by paw paws
and wild persimmons
off John Brown
on Middle Creek.

I open the envelope
of morchella spores mailed
to this urban address
far from the fauna
and fungi we hand gathered—
filling baskets
in family woodland
surrounding a 1908 farmhouse,
planted at the end

of the field a decade
before the last epidemic.

I think of city deer here
feeding at the edges
on the mushrooms
that people fallen stumps
in clear-cut.
What I might find outside
beyond the tangled
brace of blackberries
should I need to forage this season?
Not the fronds we once sautéed
that are still unfurling at Ferndale,
nor the dewberries spreading
by the pond around the mile
where red-winged blackbirds
with bright epaulettes
lay blue-freckled eggs
in nests threaded through reeds—
though no one is there now
to dig gritty tubers from the cattails
and serve them roasted
with sumac tea
that puckers like tamarind.

And so I broadcast the dust
from this plastic package—
my view corralled on all sides
by the fences and houses
caught in the kitchen window
like the familiar fly—
bobbing at the pane
only it and the morels
have followed me
home

Restraint

On this stretch of street
flanked by yards of boredom
yawning wide—
every blade
stands straight
as an Eisenhower
era haircut.
Through stay-at-home
orders or quarantines,
these lawns tended
with the detail of bonsai
or a seafoam green kitchen—
the gaps between slabs
and cobble teased clean
of crabgrass; dandelions
extracted by their teeth,
and not a single pad of moss
along the sprayed drives
sealed like secrets.

But here rises one
neither sowed nor mown
with grass you could part
with both hands,
a front lot filled
with rippling thistle
shepherd's purse, purple
vetch, and quitch waving tall
around a pool turned olive
with twitching mosquitoes
as frogs speak late
into an evening
of abundant birds.
In a world of show gardens
staged showings
virtual tours
and handwriting
that says yes,
as it follows the line
to this end. A postscript:
        We stayed home.
        My mother survived.
        This was freedom

With Thanks

On April 1st, 2020, I began writing a poem a day through the first month of a pandemic lockdown, then continued into a summer filled with smoke, an autumn of global flooding, and a winter of social justice protests. It wasn't my idea. I was discovering social media twenty years late and Liz Garton Scanlon was about to post a haiku a day that April. And I thought, why not? What can we do against it, or else, shall we & why not? I knew I could manage seventeen syllables a day for a month. I found instead I could produce a page. Emily Dickinson wrote a poem a day from home, and in partial isolation, for 2,956 straight days. It was possible. Many thanks to translation editor Romina Espinosa (also a poet), for beginning the first month's writing journey with me, and to everyone who read earlier drafts of these poems—and either encouraged me to continue or refrained from advising that I cease—including Becca, Christina, Dex, Faith, Jill, Kymm, Loie, Lora, Marilyn, Michael, Mindy, Nancy, and my family.

Allison **A. deFreese** grew up on a pig farm in Kansas. She holds three cats, one GED® certificate, a liberal arts degree from Ottawa University, and three advanced degrees starting with "M." Her work also includes leading literary translation workshops for the Oregon Society of Translators and Interpreters, teaching in the University of Texas at Rio Grande Valley's virtual Master of Arts in Spanish Translation and Interpreting program, and both designing and teaching adult literacy and literature courses for Spanish speakers. Previously the recipient of a James A. Michener Writing Fellowship (thank you UT@A), an AWP Intro Award, and a National Endowment for the Arts Literature Translation Fellowship, deFreese has lived in Mexico, Bolivia, and Japan. Her recent literary translations include María Negroni's *Elegy for Joseph Cornell* (Dalkey Archive Press, 2020); José Moreno Hernández's *Soaring to New Heights: The Memoir of a Child Migrant Farmworker Who Became a NASA Astronaut* (Renuevo Press, 2020); Karla Marrufo's *Flame Trees in May* (forthcoming), and Verónica González Arredondo's *I Am Not That Body* (Pub House Books Montreal, 2020). Her book *The Night with James Dean and Other Prose Poems* won Cathexis Northwest Press's 2022 chapbook competition.